What Did One Elephant Say to the Other?

A Book About Communication

BY

BECKY BAINES

NATIONAL GEOGRAPHIC

Washington, D.C.

What did one elephant say to the other?

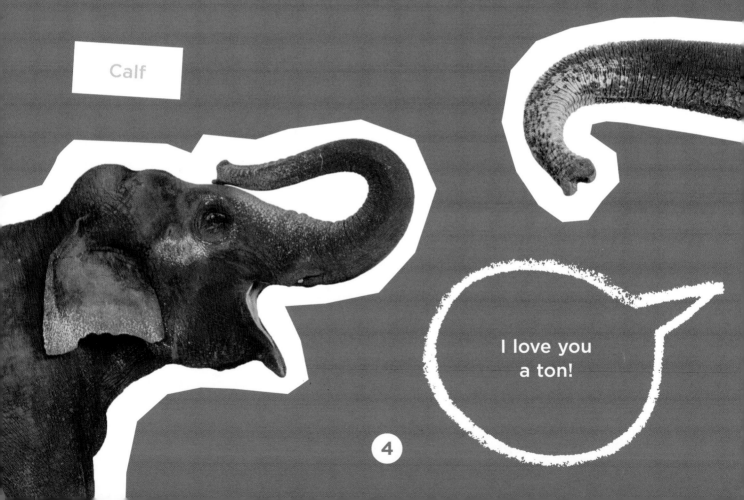

Calf

I love you
a ton!

4

Asian Elephants

African Elephants

6

With no words,
no barking,
no squawking,
elephants use their
whole bodies for talking.

Elephants live together in groups,
and have very long lives.
They have a lot to talk about!

When elephants sense danger, they wave their ears to look bigger and more threatening.

An elephant's ears slap back and forth to tell you to stay away...

porcupine

puffer fish

Other animals also try to look bigger when danger is near.

or to pick up
the sound of other
animals around
and know—is it

10

Grrrrrrr!

danger or play?

Growl!

Lions and tigers are no match for a grown elephant, but they are dangerous to calves.

11

Elephants use their long, strong trunks

Elephants use their trunks to greet other elephants by waving, touching, stroking, and smelling. Smelling is how they know who's who!

to say what's on their mind.

They can **trumpet** out loud,

Trumpeting is a loud noise elephants make. It says PAY ATTENTION.

beat the ground,

15

16

or tell calves
they're falling behind.

I'm going!

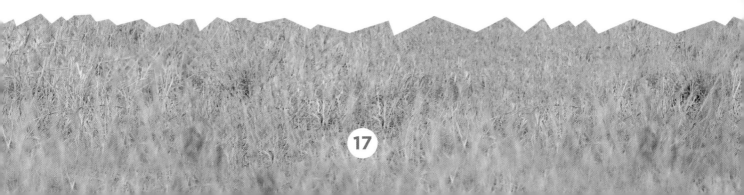

Sometimes elephants peep or grumble,

Most peeps and grumbles are just to say "I'm here."

peep

GRUMBLE

making noises loud and clear.

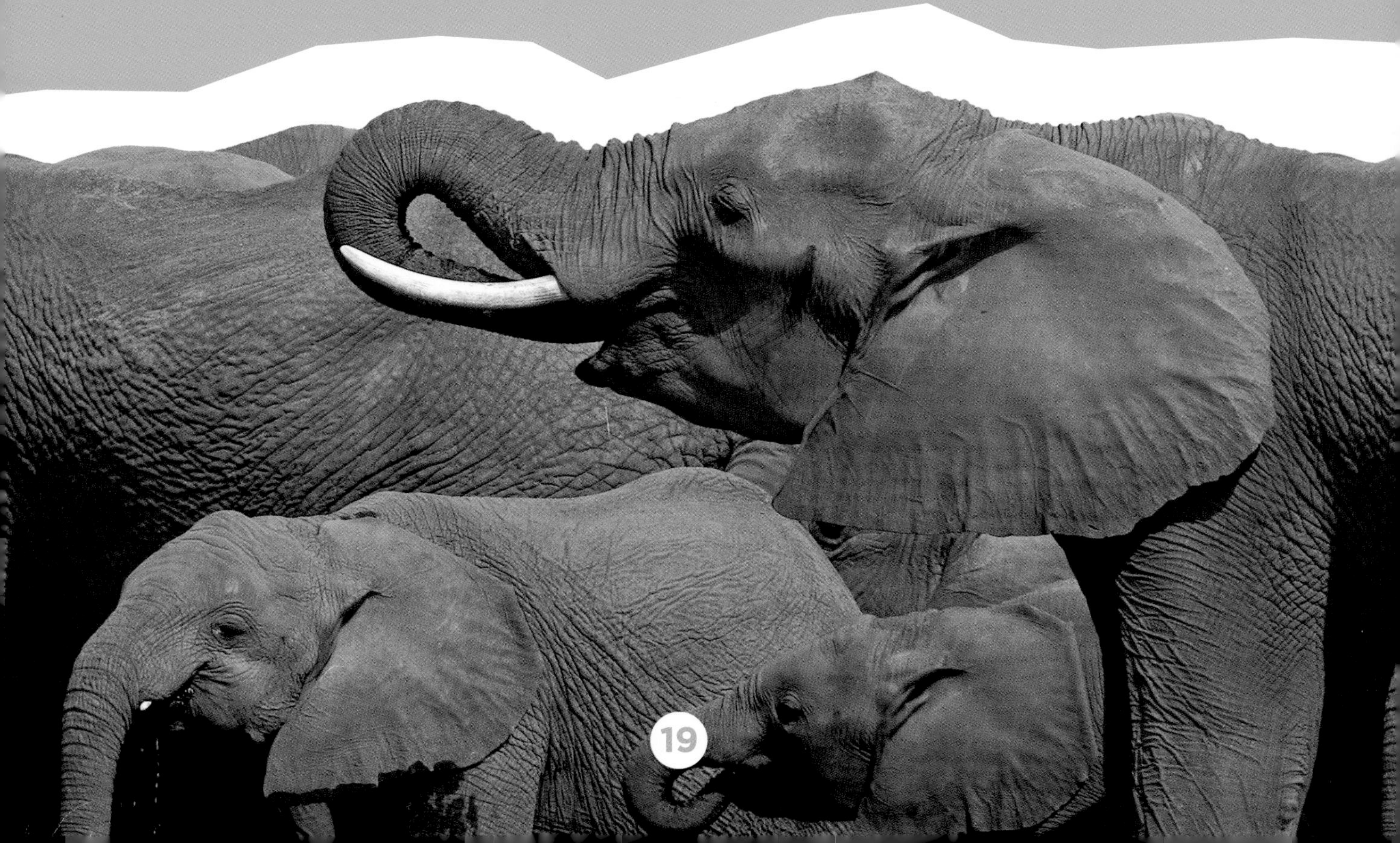

But sometimes they speak in rumbles so deep,

they make sounds that we humans can't hear.

A deep rumble travels through the ground. Scientists think elephants can hear rumbles many miles away—through their feet!

Elephant cows use their bodies to say, "Come under me, out of the sun."

And when Aunties crowd around a calf, they're saying, "You're safe, little one."

So, while elephants
don't speak the
same way we do

to say hi to
one another,

if you watch
their bodies,
you just might know

what one elephant
says to the other!

Zigzag through these ideas for more thoughts about communication.

Why don't elephants use words like people do?

Where does your voice come from?

Put a shirt worn by your Mom in a bag. Put someone else's in another bag. Without looking, see if you can smell which one's your Mom's.

If elephants lived underwater, how would they talk?

What could you do with a trunk instead of a nose?

Do you have Aunties like baby elephants do?

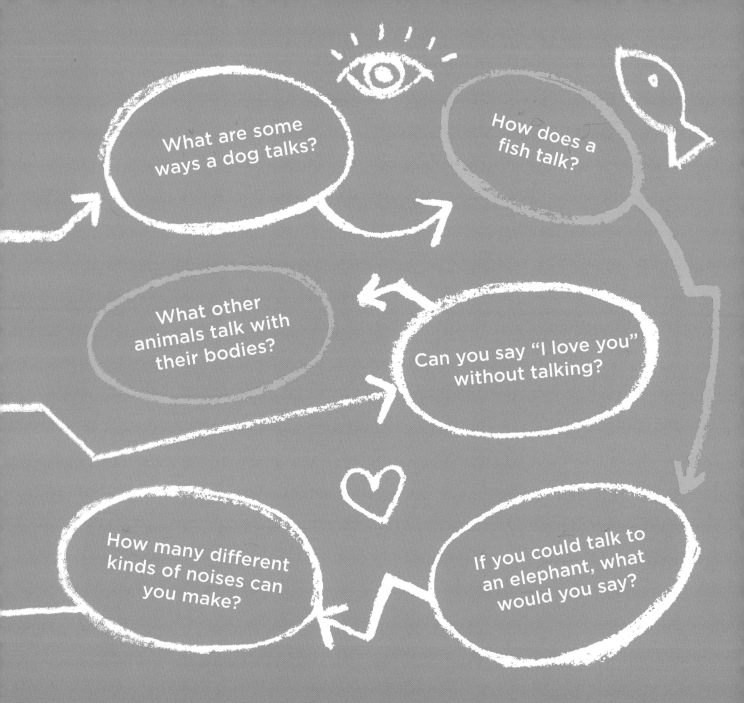

National Geographic's
net proceeds support
vital exploration,
conservation, research,
and education programs.

Published by the National Geographic Society
1145 17th Street, N.W.
Washington, D.C. 20036
Visit us online at www.nationalgeographic.com/books

Design: fuszion

Printed in the United States of America

Library of Congress Cataloging-in-Publication Data

Baines, Rebecca.
   What Did One Elephant Say to the Other? :
A Book About Communication /
by Becky Baines.
     p. cm. — (Zig zag)
   ISBN 978-1-4263-0307-4 (trade) —
ISBN 978-1-4263-0308-1 (library)
1. Animal communication. I. Title.
QL776B35 2008
591.59—dc22
2008007218

Photo Credits
Corbis: 4, 8, 20, 21, 22, 23, 24, 27
Getty Images: Cover, 5, 9, 15
iStock: 9
Beverly Joubert: 6-7, 18-19
Minden Pictures: 16, 17
Shutterstock: 14, 15

To my sister Katie
and my new brother
Morgan—who I
love a TON!
—B.B.